Original title:
Whispers in the Woods

Copyright © 2025 Creative Arts Management OÜ
All rights reserved.

Author: Benjamin Caldwell
ISBN HARDBACK: 978-1-80567-160-2
ISBN PAPERBACK: 978-1-80567-459-7

The Language of Leaves in the Breeze

Leaves gossip softly, all in a rush,
They gossip about squirrels, and oh, the hush.
A dance with the wind, oh what a sight,
Leaves mutter secrets, in pure delight.

Branches do wiggle, like they've got a clove,
Each rustle a giggle, secrets they wove.
The trunks nod knowingly, a tree's little jest,
As acorns roll by, they're surely the best.

Hushed Stories of the Bark and Earth

The bark tells tales, with lines like a map,
Of critters and beetles, and a cheeky chap.
Fungi chime in, with hats and a grin,
Spores flying high, let the stories begin!

The earth hums beneath, with a ticklish laugh,
Where roots play tag, in their tangled half.
A ladybug winks, on a mushroom high,
While ants take a trip, under the sky.

Flickers of Light in the Gloom

Fireflies dancing, like stars on a spree,
Flashing their smiles, just for you and me.
The shadows giggle, as they start to creep,
While owls hoot softly, the woods in sleep.

Moonbeams tickle branches, with a soft embrace,
Laughter in silence, in this funny place.
A fox sneaks out, with a twinkle so bright,
He's plotting a party, oh what a night!

Lullabies of the Woodland Spirits

Little sprites giggle, on the edge of the night,
Singing their tunes, oh what a delight!
They twirl 'round the ferns, in a whirlwind show,
A chirp here and there, just to let you know.

Mossy cushions whisper, come take a seat,
Join in the laughter, with roots at your feet.
While shadows chuckle, they tap dance away,
Woodland spirits giggling, till the break of day.

Tranquil Tales Beneath the Moonlit Path

The owls are hooting, tickling the trees,
Squirrels dance like they've had too much cheese.
A raccoon is laughing, hiding its stash,
While fireflies twinkle and twirl in a flash.

Beneath the bright moon, shadows take flight,
Chasing each other in a playful night.
A chipmunk plays poker, cards all askew,
The stakes, just some acorns, a nutty crew.

Shadows Telling Stories Untold

Bats are the comedians, swooping around,
Telling tall tales with each twist and sound.
A fox prances by in his fanciest hat,
While a turtle debates who is faster— a cat.

Leaves flutter down like confetti in glee,
As lizards perform in a dance, oh so free.
A deer sips some tea, gossiping loud,
While the crickets all chuckle, forming a crowd.

The Gathering of Gentle Spirits

In the hush of the night, the sprites convene,
With giggles as soft as a gentle spring green.
One sprightly spirit spills tea on a shoe,
While others all tease 'bout the clumsy one too.

A toad on a log croaks out a sage rhyme,
While the trees sway in rhythm, lost in their prime.
They dance with delight, what a quirky affair,
Even mushrooms join in, with their tops in the air.

Whispers of the Trail Less Taken

Down the less traveled path, what will we find?
A hedgehog in tutus, one of a kind!
With snorts and with giggles, the critters unite,
As they march in a line, oh, what a sight!

A rabbit plays DJ, spinning that tune,
While fireflies flash like a disco ball moon.
They shimmy and shake, in a joyous parade,
In the heart of the night, none are afraid.

Harmonies of the Hidden Path

In the shadows, squirrels dance,
Giggling leaves, they take a chance.
Bouncing logs and frogs that croak,
Trees are laughing, what a joke!

Crazy mushrooms, hats askew,
A wandering snail says, "Look at you!"
Chasing shadows, we all fall,
Frolicking critters heed the call.

A raccoon's mask, so debonair,
Sneaks to snatch a berry, unaware.
Tickling plants with playful grins,
Nature's jesters, joy begins!

The forest hums a silly tune,
Bouncing breezes, whispers soon.
Every rustle holds a cheer,
In this wild place, smiles appear!

Secrets of the Sylvan Realm

Beneath the ferns, a frog does sing,
Bright-eyed beetles join the fling.
They do the cha-cha, if you please,
While ants march by with perfect ease.

Nutty squirrels, quite the show,
Steal each acorn in a row.
Running circles, over the ground,
In their antics, laughter's found.

Mice play tag with nimble feet,
Chasing shadows, what a treat!
In this spot, no frown's allowed,
Silly critters dance so proud.

A hedgehog rolled, oh what a sight,
Twirling 'round, a comical fright.
Nature's stage, with joy and play,
In this realm, we laugh away!

Gentle Thoughts Beneath the Branches

Beneath the branches, shadows prance,
Chubby rabbits take a chance.
Twirling grass, so green and bright,
Bunnies giggle in delight!

The wind's a jokester, pulling trees,
With silly whispers, little tease.
Knocking acorns on my head,
Nature's humor, laughter spread.

A turtle grins, moves slow but sure,
While butterflies flit and stir.
Every petal's got a grin,
In this paradise, joy begins.

Tiny ants dress up in style,
Skipping stones, they do it with a smile.
Amid the roots and branches fair,
Mirth is found with every air!

Serenades of Mossy Stones

On mossy stones, a band does play,
Rocky raccoons start the sway.
With tiny flutes and panpipes near,
Their tunes tickle the ear with cheer.

The owls hoot in silly rhymes,
Echoing through the leafy climes.
A badger struts, all dressed in twirls,
Nature's night, filled with giggles and swirls.

Skipper bugs with little hats,
Dancing 'round with all the rats.
In the moonlight, shadows draw,
Each rustling leaf just makes us guffaw.

The fireflies blink, a disco light,
Toadstools bounce, what a sight!
Each note dances, wild and free,
In this haven, fun's the key!

Resonance of the Rushing River

The river sings a silly tune,
Its splashy dance makes frogs commune.
With every ripple, jokes are tossed,
A fish jumped high, and laughter lost.

The ducks all quack in harmony,
Clumsy splashes, a sight to see.
A beaver builds with silly style,
While otters glide, they laugh a while.

The water's voice, a bubbly cheer,
Each stone a listener, never sheer.
The current slips with playful glee,
A prankster stream, it tickles me.

So come and dip your toes awhile,
In nature's jest, we find a smile.
The rushing river, loud and bright,
Is a stage for fun, from morn till night.

The Silence of Shimmering Leaves

Leaves gossip softly in the breeze,
They share the juiciest stories with ease.
A squirrel eavesdrops, tail a-twitch,
While sunbeams play, causing a glitch.

A curious crow caws out a pun,
As acorns tumble, oh what fun!
The branches shake with secret mirth,
A ticklish rustle brings light to earth.

Underneath, the grass rolls its eyes,
While ants parade in tiny ties.
A swift wind carries giggles around,
As nature chuckles without a sound.

In leafy halls, the silence speaks,
Of playful critters, hide-and-seek.
A moment here is pure delight,
As shimmering leaves take flight.

Echoes of the Hidden Glade

In the glade, a laugh resounds,
Where shadows twist and fun abounds.
A rabbit hops, with ears so tall,
And snickers bounce from wall to wall.

The shadows whisper jokes, quite neat,
As hedgehogs giggle on their feet.
Mushrooms sprout in silly postures,
As nature pleads, 'Join in my rosters!'

A deer trips up, in graceful stride,
And butterflies dance, filled with pride.
The glade's a stage, a merry sight,
Where every creature finds pure light.

So linger here, let chuckles flow,
In hidden nooks where laughter grows.
Nature's echoes, bright and free,
Transform this space to jubilee.

Soft Secrets of the Sylvan Realm

In leafy halls where shadows play,
The squirrels hold a grand buffet.
They dance and leap, munching nuts,
While giggling softly, just for laughs.

A rabbit in a polka-dot tie,
Tries to impress the girl nearby.
He slips on mud, takes quite the fall,
And all the critters laugh and call.

The owl, wise with spectacles on,
Critiques their style, 'Oh, come on!
Your dance moves lack a certain flair,
Just waddle, hop, with flair to spare!'

A chipmunk raps, a fox beats drums,
Making tunes, oh how it hums!
Nature's stage, under moonlight's gleam,
Where all join in, a wild dream.

Interludes of the Underbrush

In crowded bushes, secrets brew,
A hedgehog recites a joke or two.
The bees buzz in to catch the punch,
But trip on petals, oh what a crunch!

The badger sings a silly song,
While butterflies flutter along.
They land on snouts, which makes them sneeze,
And send the ants into a tease!

A raccoon juggles acorns high,
While fireflies twinkle in the sky.
Suddenly, he drops them down,
And scurries off, a frantic clown.

Thus life unfolds beneath the trees,
With hearty laughs and friendly tease.
In every rustle, fun's revealed,
Where nature's humor is unsealed!

Voices Carried on the Breeze

Amidst the leaves, a chatter arises,
A cricket's joke, oh, how it surprises!
He brags he can play the tambourine,
But slips on dew, falls, it's quite the scene!

The owl can't stop with laughter loud,
While the fox struts, feeling proud.
"I'm the best dancer!" he prances fast,
But faces a bee and runs at last!

A squirrel points, "Oh look at him,
That dance was surely far from grim!"
The forest echoes with such delight,
As giggles twirl throughout the night.

Through ticklish grass, the laughter flows,
As every critter shares their woes.
Funny tales under the moon's stage,
Nature's drama, all the rage!

Chronicles of the Hidden Glade

In a glade where sunlight winks,
A mouse debates with skunk that stinks.
"Your scent's a weapon, a fierce embrace!"
"Just try to outrun me in this race!"

The frogs are croaking silly tunes,
While plump toads hop; who'll catch the moons?
A snail's slow dance brings giggles near,
As he slowly polishes a beer!

A woodpecker tells tales of fame,
Claiming fame from a famous name.
But every peck on the old oak,
Turns into a giggling joke!

These chronicles of silly sounds,
Frolic and tumble on merry grounds.
In nature's book, the fun won't fade,
Where laughter's cast and joy displayed.

The Quietude Before Dawn's Arrival

Beneath the stars, no one can hear,
A squirrel's snack attack, it's very near.
The crickets play their sweet little tune,
While owls are plotting to steal a prune.

The rabbit hops to see the show,
It's not brave, just a little slow.
A rustle, a chase, and what a sight,
A raccoon joins in for the late-night flight.

By dawn's first light, what a circus grand,
Nature's jesters, they all take a stand.
With sleepy yawns, the night takes its bow,
As sunlight splashes on all of us now.

Secrets Dancing on a Gentle Breeze

There's gossip among the leaves, so sly,
A flutter, a rustle, oh my, oh my!
The robins chirp, sharing tales of delight,
Of worms in a latte, what a bold bite!

The breeze, it giggles, tickles the trees,
As squirrels conspire with the buzzing bees.
They plot little pranks, what a funny sight,
While shadows play games till the moon takes flight.

The flowers all nod, they can hardly keep in,
With secrets like these, where do we begin?
A daisy might tell if you listen real close,
But tattle-tales get swatted with a rose.

Conversations with the Wind-Stirred Grasses

The grasses sway like they've got a plan,
They tickle my toes, as best as they can.
One blade says, 'Look, it's a cow on the run!'
While others just giggle, their work is such fun!

A rabbit chimes in, 'I heard it's a race,'
While moles underground are all just in place.
The larks overhead sing truths quite absurd,
Of how worms can dance, oh haven't you heard?

With whispers of giggles from green to the sky,
These grasses hold secrets, they know how to fly.
While I join the chatter, a laugh on the breeze,
In this patch of green, I'd rather not leave.

Glances from the Glooming Foliage

In shadows deep, the trunks are quite bold,
Outrageous stories, so many retold.
The thorns roll their eyes at the vines overhead,
'Less chit-chat, more action,' they tease with dread.

The bushes gossip, with blooms that can't wait,
While shadows play tag, isn't this first rate?
A bear passes by, looking rather bemused,
Wondering why he's so often confused.

The owls hoot loudly, spreading wild tales,
Of nighttime whoops and raccoon trails.
So next time you stroll, have a look all around,
For the foliage keeps secrets, oh so profound!

Traces of the Forgotten

Once I found a shoe, all alone,
Its mate was lost, on a journey unknown.
It seemed to giggle, caught in a tree,
Saying, 'Can't you see? I dance wild and free!'

Squirrels in hats threw a wild tea bash,
With acorns as cups, they'd giggle and clash.
Rabbits in bow ties, sipping on dew,
Claiming, 'This party? It's all about you!'

The Enigma of Silent Beasts

A bear in a tutu, trying to twirl,
Spinning around, causing quite a whirl.
His friends, the deer, just couldn't stop laughing,
'Look at him go!' while gently rafts passing.

An owl wore glasses, reading at night,
Saying, 'To fly? That's a whole lot of fright!'
Raccoons debated which snack is the best,
'Pine nuts or berries? Let's put it to quest!'

Murmurs on the Path to Nowhere

A path of tickles covered in leaves,
Where even the trees let out little heaves.
'The wind just told me a joke!' said a fox,
'What do you call a tree with no socks?'

The mushrooms giggled, painted in spots,
'We're not just fungi; we're dancing hot pots!'
While crickets chirped in a syncopated beat,
Saying, 'Step right up, join this wild treat!'

The Soft Embrace of Misty Mornings

In the mist of dawn, a rabbit sat tight,
Wrapped in soft clouds, a fluffy delight.
He snuggled a snail, claiming, 'You're my friend,'
They plotted a race, right down to the bend.

A hedgehog joined in, wearing a crown,
Saying, 'I'm the king, let's not bring a frown!'
With laughter and joy, they danced in the dew,
Morning giggles echoed, as all creatures drew.

The Rustle of Time in the Thicket

In the thicket where squirrels roam,
Every branch seems like a busy phone.
Trees gossip as leaves swirl around,
Even the grass can't keep from being profound.

A hedgehog sings his prickly tune,
While frogs croak softly, a funny boon.
Time flows like a stream, quick and light,
Yet rabbits dash, thinking it's night!

The owls hoot jokes from their perch,
While ants throw a party under the birch.
The wind carries tales, some fishy and loud,
As critters convene, feeling proud.

Amidst the dance of clashing scents,
Laughter erupts, it's nature's events.
With every rustle, a chuckle is found,
In this thicket, joy rings all around.

The Quiet Dance of Shadows

Shadows waltz under the moon's soft glow,
A raccoon in a tuxedo steals the show.
Bats twirl by, doing loops in the air,
While the owl rolls its eyes, finding it rare.

The mushrooms giggle as the fox tiptoes,
In the twilight's ballroom where nobody knows.
A beetle breaks out in a disco groove,
While the dust bunnies hop—can't help but move!

The trees sway slowly, joining the fun,
Their branches waving like a well-done run.
Every shadow a partner, every leaf a beat,
In this hidden hall, life feels complete.

As the night fades, the dance slows down,
With sleepy sighs, each creature wears a crown.
In the quiet arms of the starlit beams,
They tuck in tight, drifting into dreams.

Phrases Played by the Wind

The wind carries tales from the distant glade,
Tickling the leaves, in games that they played.
A rusted tin can joins in the fun,
Singing of adventures under the sun.

The daisies gossip with their petals wide,
Sharing secrets with the passing tide.
A squirrel shimmies, tries to keep pace,
While a butterfly giggles, lost in the race.

Branches clap hands, celebrating the day,
As mushrooms snap selfies, not fading away.
The pine trees chuckle, their needles all dance,
In this playful madness, they seize every chance.

With every gust, a new jest takes flight,
The night hums along, all feels just right.
Nature's a jester, with glee and mirth,
In the game of existence, we find our worth.

Secrets Shared Among the Saplings

In a circle of saplings, secrets unfold,
With giggles and whispers, some shy and bold.
A crow caws loudly, but it's just a tease,
While ladybugs gather, aiming to please.

Each sapling leans in, sharing a plot,
About the big trees and the lessons they've got.
A beetle offers wisdom, slight and spry,
"Don't rush to grow up, give it a try!"

The roots interlace, making a chain,
As they swap stories through puddles of rain.
A gentle breeze tickles each trunk with flair,
Life's sweet little secrets swirl in the air.

Come twilight, the tales fade, but the bond stays tight,
As starlight twinkles, all feels just right.
In the grove of young dreams, laughter is free,
Sharing those secrets, just nature and we.

Echoing Heartbeats of the Earth

In the shady grove, a squirrel sips tea,
Telling tales of acorns, wild and free.
The trees lean close, eavesdropping tight,
While rabbits plan their next dance tonight.

A chipmunk juggles nuts with great flair,
While nearby, a deer has too much hair.
Raccoons chuckle, plotting their scheme,
As the sun sets low, they're ready to dream.

The owl hoots jokes, a wise guy at heart,
His punchlines echo, a clever art.
Creatures laugh, their laughter cascades,
In nature's theatre, where joy never fades.

Under the stars, ridiculous sighs,
The moon winks down, with sparkling eyes.
Together they giggle, the night feels right,
In this woodland haven, what a delight!

The Subtle Breeze of Secrets

A breeze glides by, with secrets to share,
It tickles the flowers, ruffles their hair.
A butterfly whispers, with wings like a fan,
While bees sell gossip from flower to plan.

The grasses swish in playful delight,
A worm gives a wink, what a charming sight!
The wind blows softly, a playful decree,
"Can we dance, dear critters, just wait and see!"

A hedgehog hums, making quite the tune,
While frogs croak choruses beneath the moon.
Laughter erupts from under the leaves,
As nature's orchestra happily weaves.

Underneath branches, secrets unwind,
In this quirky realm, hilarity's kind.
The forest delights, with its charming spree,
As laughter and whispers immerse wild and free.

Trail of the Unspoken

Along the path where shadows grow long,
A fox tries to sing, but gets it all wrong.
He trills out a tune, much to his shame,
While the birds all giggle, playing their game.

A tortoise races, slow but precise,
He thinks he's a rocket, all decked out in spice.
But who's keeping track? It's a whimsical race,
With friends cheering loud, what a funny base!

A deer trips over roots, makes quite the scene,
While nearby a fish critiques, looking keen.
"Just jump!" calls a rabbit, laughter ensues,
In this untamed theater where kindness muzzles blues.

On this trail of giggles, unspoken delight,
Nature composes its grand comedy night.
In rustling leaves, the fun echoes clear,
As the critters unite with a cheery cheer!

Nature's Gentle Cadence

The rhythm of life in nature's embrace,
A snail dances slow, with elegant grace.
While ants do the tango, in precise lines,
And butterflies flutter, marking their signs.

A woodpecker knocks, like a drummer so bold,
While frogs croak along, though their voices are old.
Together they bop in delightful parade,
Each step in tune, as friendships are made.

The flowers sway gently, a sway to the beat,
Bouncing to laughter, from head to tiny feet.
The sun lends a wink, grinning so wide,
As nature forgets not to laugh at the ride.

In this cadence of mirth, life blossoms bright,
With joy in each rustle, under the soft light.
In harmony woven, they spin tales so grand,
An orchestra of giggles, in this playful land!

Subtle Tales Among the Twigs

In the forest, squirrels plot,
Chasing acorns, are they fraught?
While the rabbits play their tricks,
Painting tales with little licks.

The owls hoot with great delight,
A disco party in the night.
But don't tell the deer, they're shy,
Bouncing quietly as they fly.

Raccoons dance in shadows deep,
Stealing snacks while others sleep.
A bear waltzes, oh, so bold,
Wearing leaves like fashion gold.

So listen close when shadows stir,
The trees giggle, oh, what a blur!
The pines share secrets, wild and free,
A comedy act for you and me.

The Calm Whisper of Rustling Grass

The grass giggles in the breeze,
Tickling toes of ants with ease.
Crickets play a tune so sly,
As butterflies swirl and fly.

A snail moves at a snail's pace,
Revealing its curious face.
While frogs croak their jokes so loud,
They're the laughter of the crowd.

Bees are buzzing in a rush,
Wearing pollen, looking plush.
But don't ask the blooms, they'll moan,
They'd rather chat with seeds they've sown.

Listen to the grass that sways,
In quiet giggles, it displays.
Through the meadow, fun does pass,
In the calm of rustling grass.

Hidden Hues of the Forest

A magpie sports a beak of gold,
With secrets of the forest told.
Leaves gossip in shades so bright,
Dancing colors, pure delight.

Mushrooms wear their polka dots,
In parties where the gnome plots.
They spin tales 'round trees so wide,
Underneath, the critters hide.

Fungi jive with fungus friends,
In a game that never ends.
But watch your step, oh, be so wise,
For a toadstool might just disguise!

The trees, they chuckle, oh-so-sweet,
As scampering tails skip to the beat.
Such vibrant quirks, such playful hues,
In the forest, joy ensues.

Murmurs from the Underbrush

From below, the whispers rise,
An army of critters in disguise.
Grasshoppers launch a stand-up show,
As crickets crack jokes, going toe-to-toe.

The hedgehog rolls in lopsided glee,
While snails share stories of their tea.
A wise old fox takes the floor,
With knock-knock jokes, they'll all adore.

The thorns giggle in the dark,
While fireflies join with a spark.
Even the rocks can't help but grin,
As all the woodland laughs begin.

So if you hear a rustling laugh,
Don't be alarmed, take a photograph.
The underbrush is never shy,
It's a venue where good times fly.

Echoes of the Enchanted Grove

In a grove where squirrels chatter,
Frogs belch tunes that really matter.
Rabbits dance in silly flocks,
While owls plot their nightly socks.

Every leaf has a giggle stored,
Tree trunks seem to laugh, bored.
Acorns roll like tiny balls,
Mice script plays on forest walls.

The brook chuckles at the jest,
Turtles take their time, no stress.
Breezes tickle all that's green,
Nature's humor, bright and keen.

At dusk, the critters share a grin,
As fireflies dress in sparkly skin.
It's a party nobody knows,
In this grove where laughter flows.

Murmurs of the Canopy

Leaves are jiving, having fun,
Chasing shadows in the sun.
Branches sway with mischievous glee,
Speaking secrets amongst the tree.

Caterpillars wear tiny hats,
While raccoons avoid the chitchats.
Squirrels play hide and seek with pride,
As lively bunnies hop alongside.

Every beam of sunlight beams,
On tree trunks plotting silly schemes.
The wind, a comedian unseen,
Makes the flowers giggle and glean.

At dusk the critters start to play,
Forming jokes in their own way.
Laughter echoes through each leaf,
In a forest of humor and belief.

Secrets Beneath the Ancient Boughs

Beneath the boughs so thick and strong,
Where creatures gather all day long.
Secret meetings where they chat,
A wise old owl wears a party hat.

Ants debate on passing crumbs,
While crickets tap their tiny drums.
A badger rants about the rain,
As hedgehogs complain of walking pain.

A leaf lets slip a giggling story,
Of frogs in suits, all dressed in glory.
Mice conduct a choir of squeaks,
Their melody puts the forest to sleep.

With every rustle, laughter spreads,
In the night, the fun never treads.
The ancient trees nod with delight,
As secrets bloom beneath the night.

The Silent Song of the Forest

Quietly, the woods do hum,
To the beat of a squirrel's drum.
Beetles march in parade line,
As mushrooms sip on sweet moonshine.

A sleepy owl can't stop its yawns,
While frogs hop about in funny pawns.
Trees confess to passing winds,
Their jokes are where the laughter begins.

Fireflies put on a glowing show,
While the crickets compose a flow.
As shadows frolic with delight,
The moon tickles everything in sight.

In the forest where giggles soar,
Nature's jesters always adore.
In the night, joy's sweet refrain,
Keeps the woodland spirits entertained.

Shadows Dance Among the Foliage

Under trees where shadows play,
Squirrels gossip all the day.
A rabbit snickers, 'What a sight!'
The fox just winks and takes to flight.

Mushrooms giggle, sprouting wide,
A dancing toadstool is their guide.
Leaves crackle with a giggly cheer,
Nature's jesters, loud and clear.

Frogs croak jokes that never end,
At every turn, a playful bend.
The breeze tosses leaves like confetti,
In this woodland fiesta, oh so petty!

Beneath the boughs, let laughter flow,
As nature's tricksters steal the show.
Here, in this forest of bright delight,
The shadows dance, taking flight.

The Language of Leaves

The leaves converse in rustling tones,
About their crush on crunchy bones.
An acorn laughs, 'I'm feeling bold!'
While twigs exchange tales of old.

Breezes giggle, swaying low,
As branches bend in breezy flow.
A pinecone raps, "I'm quite the star!"
While cedar murmurs, "Not by far!"

Dancing petals, in a whirl,
Find ways to tickle and to twirl.
They whisper secrets, oh so sly,
While squirrels roll their eyes and sigh.

In every crackle, every twist,
A woodland comedy can't be missed.
So listen close, let laughter weave,
In this chatty glen where leaves believe.

Beneath the Veil of Pines

Underneath the piney gaze,
A bear complains in funny ways.
He wore a hat, too small, too bright,
The trees are laughing, what a sight!

Beneath the bows, a rabbit pranced,
In polka dots, he took a chance.
He tripped on roots, let out a squeal,
The pines chuckled, 'What a deal!'

A woodpecker's drumming starts the show,
A rhythm funny, fast, and slow.
He's got the moves, the dance of wood,
While creatures nod, and all is good.

Amidst the laughter, tales unwind,
Where every nutty dream's aligned.
So come and play beneath the pines,
Where humor grows and mischief shines.

Hushed Tales of the Timberlands

In the timberlands where secrets creep,
A chipmunk's story puts you to sleep.
He talks of snacks and nutty grace,
And mountain lions keeping pace.

A raccoon shares a midnight theft,
With such charm, you're truly left.
He winks and says, 'I'm quite the pro!'
His forest friends erupt in 'Whoah!'

Owl's wisdom is a comical sight,
He hoots of hiccups in the night.
With head turned sideways, wise yet sly,
He makes the owlets laugh and cry.

So gather round, let laughter ring,
In timberlands, there's joy to bring.
Each tale a twist, a funny twist,
In the forest's heart, it can't be missed.

Fables of the Forgotten Path

In the forest, squirrels wear hats,
Plotting mischief, and stealing cat snacks.
They giggle and chatter, oh what a sight,
As mushrooms stand tall, feeling quite spright.

A hedgehog with glasses reads tales by the stream,
While rabbits hold poker nights, living the dream.
The trees peek and listen, with branches that sway,
As giggles echo louder, they're here to stay.

The Call of Dappled Shadows

Beneath leafy arches, the sunlight does play,
A raccoon plays drums; it's his favorite way.
The owls roll their eyes, "Oh, not this again,"
As the fox tries to jiggle, he's tripped by a hen.

The shadows have secrets, a mischievous grin,
While toads keep the rhythm, tapping their skin.
A party of critters, wild laughs fill the air,
In dappled light laughter, they dance without care.

Hidden Harmonies of Evergreen

A squirrel in a vest plays the trumpet, quite bold,
While pine cones compose, a story untold.
The hedgehogs tap dance in shoes made of leaves,
And the rabbits engage in wild make-believes.

The melodies bubble, like sap in the trees,
Each twig has a story, each rustle a tease.
The ferns sway in rhythm—nature's delight,
In a world of their crafting, it feels just right.

An Ode to Mossy Silence

Upon the soft ground, the turtles trade jokes,
While the moss stretches slow, as it gently provokes.
The owls start to chuckle, their eyes wide with cheer,
As mushrooms giggle softly, with nothing to fear.

A snail in a bowtie tells tales of his race,
While beetles take selfies, all smiles on their face.
In this quiet domain, with laughter so light,
Mossy silence, in jest, brings joy to the night.

The Still Path of Broken Sunlight

Squirrels in a frantic race,
Chasing shadows, lost in space.
Sunbeams tickle rusty leaves,
While laughter hides beneath the eaves.

A rabbit jumps, a branch does snap,
Startled, he spins, falls in a lap.
With a thud, the world does pause,
Nature chuckles, and cheers applause.

Pinecones roll like bowling balls,
Underfoot, the forest calls.
Mushrooms nod in glee and jest,
Telling tales of their grand quest.

But in the stillness, watch your feet,
For rooty traps can't be beat!
The path may lead to giggling blooms,
In broken sunlight, joy resumes.

Glistening Murmurs on Dewy Mornings

The grass wears pearls, all tucked in tight,
While dragonflies dance, oh what a sight!
Ants host a party, with crumbs as treats,
Beneath the big oak, they gather sweet feats.

A froggy croaks, in his fancy hat,
Disproving rumors of being fat.
With every leap, he bounces dreams,
As morning giggles in glistening beams.

The sun peeks through, a golden tease,
Bees buzz along, in a playful breeze.
They tickle the flowers, make them sway,
And fashion a dance that brightens the day.

Every droplet shares a joke,
With sparkles that burst, as if they spoke.
For nature's laughter rings so clear,
On dewy mornings filled with cheer.

Leaves Like Lullabies in the Breezes

Leaves rustle softly, secrets unfold,
Tales of mischief, brave and bold.
A caterpillar sipping tea,
Whispers of how it might soon be free.

Swaying branches, a gentle sway,
Turning the mundane to a play.
A chubby raccoon, in slumber deep,
Dreams of snacks, while others peep.

Clouds drift along, a cheeky crew,
Puffing up shapes, some fun and new.
"Is that a dragon?" one child would sigh,
While ants march on by, just passing by.

In the breezes, laughter flows,
As nature's music playfully grows.
With each leaf a story, a tune, a cheer,
In the soft rustle, the joy draws near.

Serenades From the Shadowed Glade

In the shadowed glade, a tune is spun,
Where mushrooms wiggle, having fun.
A woodpecker pecks a silly beat,
While owls roll their eyes, it can't be beat!

A fox with flair struts like a star,
Dancing in circles, not going far.
Each paw makes rhythms that tickle the floor,
While shadows chuckle at the show and more.

Fireflies blink like jesters bright,
Joining the fun, what a delightful sight!
Twirling and swirling, they light the space,
As laughter casts a gleeful grace.

In this glade of giggles, secrets weave,
Nature and whimsy, hard to believe.
So, come join us, don't delay,
In the serenades where the fairies play.

Enigmas of the Enchanted Grove

Underneath the leafy crown,
Squirrels plot to steal a crown.
Fairy lights in mischief glow,
Chasing shadows to and fro.

A raccoon with a shiny prize,
Thinks he's clever, oh so wise.
But the owl, with a knowing wink,
Plans to catch him—oh, I think!

Breezes blow with laughter bright,
Tickling leaves till they take flight.
Mushrooms dance beneath the trees,
Singing songs of great unease.

Tales of antics in the air,
Every critter's got a flair.
In this grove, there's jokes galore,
Nature's giggles, we explore.

Voices Linger in Twilight

In the dusk, the frogs perform,
Croaking tunes that break the norm.
Fireflies flash like tiny stars,
Dancing dreams from near to far.

A rabbit hops with fancy feet,
Where the path and shadows meet.
Hesitation in his eyes,
"What's that rustling?" he replies.

Owls hoot wisdom, sounding wise,
"Relax, buddy, it's just the flies!"
Yet the rustle grows much near,
Tripping squirrels bring their cheer.

The trees giggle, swaying low,
Such strange antics stealing show.
In this night, mischief blooms,
Nature's fun, amidst the glooms.

Trails of the Timid Breathers

Little feet on a woodland trail,
Giggling hard, their faces pale.
"Did you hear that?" one frets near,
"It's just a bear, I end my cheer!"

A squirrel dressed in acorn flair,
Dances like he has no care.
"Follow me, I know the way!"
But all refuse, afraid to play.

The tall grass whispers low and sweet,
Bugs march by on tiny feet.
Daisies blink with happy glee,
"Enjoy the fright, just let it be!"

In their hearts, the fun resides,
Even if the fear abides.
Through the maze of ferns and twigs,
Forest laughter softly digs.

The Soft Hush of Nature's Breath

In the stillness, secrets spin,
A gopher dreams of fitting in.
With a hat made from a leaf,
He prances forth, despite the grief.

Badgers gossip, tails in twist,
"Did you see that? A big-eared mist!"
They point to nothing, giggle mad,
Finding joy in what they had.

The bees hum tunes of BBQ,
Tickling everyone who flew.
"Mind the thorns, they're out to play,
But join the feast, don't stray away!"

With each sound, a laughter bursts,
As night unfolds, the joy immerses.
In nature's hush, it's clear to see,
The whimsy rules, and sets us free.

Murmurs of the Ancient Trees

In the shade where squirrels play,
Old oaks gossip night and day,
Their branches laugh, a leafy grin,
As raccoons plot their next big win.

The saplings listen with wide eyes,
To tales of birds and tiny spies,
A woodpecker taps out its tune,
While rhododendrons hum in June.

Roots entwined like silly friends,
Tickling each other, making amends,
"Who's growing taller?" they jest in jest,
In this wood, it's a tree's quest!

So take a stroll and join the prank,
Where branches sway, and laughter clanks,
These ancient giants spin a yarn,
In leafy robes, they laugh and charm.

Shadows of Silent Sentinels

The pines stand tall, a watchful crew,
With every breeze, they're swaying too,
"Is that a bear? Or just a rock?"
They tease each other with playful shock.

Birches giggle in the light,
Dancing white with all their might,
"Stand still!" they mock the shy old fir,
"Your grumpy face is quite a stir!"

The sunlight tickles through the leaves,
Causing shadows to pull up sleeves,
"Dance with us!" the ferns do plea,
"Or are you too stiff — oh tree, oh tree?"

Their jokes go on till nightfall calls,
As crickets join with chirps and falls,
Together they spin a swirling glee,
Even the shadows laugh carefree.

The Quiet Song of Ferns

Ferns in green, with fronds so light,
Sway gently, not a fuss in sight,
"Hey, did you hear the joke on bark?"
They snicker softly in the dark.

"Why did the tree get so bored?
Because it couldn't find a board!"
They ripple with laughter, tickled still,
As moonlight casts its silver thrill.

Mossy partners join the fun,
With every giggle, they're all won,
The ladybug laughs in her quaint entourage,
Joining the ferns with a tiny mirage.

So dance with me, oh leafy friends,
Let's twist till the sky descends,
In quiet cubbies, we'll find our way,
To spin silly tales till the break of day.

Beneath the Boughs of Mystery

Underneath the canopy's delight,
Squirrels hold meetings, plotting their flight,
"Where's that acorn?!" one will shout,
While branches chuckle, waving about.

A turtle wanders, slow and grand,
As fern leaves whisper, "We'll make a stand!"
"Race you to the pond!" a young mouse dared,
While the wise old owl simply stared.

The snickers float on a gentle breeze,
As hedgehogs roll with unkempt ease,
"Did you hear about the old dead log?
It's a famous spot for all the frogs!"

And as the sun dips low in the sky,
The woodland creatures wave goodbye,
In their secret world, so lively and free,
Where laughter echoes, joyfully.

Echoing Footsteps Through the Thicket

In the thicket where shadows play,
Squirrels gossip about the day.
They scurry fast, they chatter loud,
While a lost shoe seeks its crowd.

Frogs jump high to catch a fly,
Bouncing here, they never shy.
Raccoons dance with mischief bright,
Underneath the silver light.

The trees have ears, or so they say,
They laugh at all who lose their way.
Birds tweet secrets, chirps so sweet,
While the path keeps shifting feet.

Here, in the thicket with its charm,
Every wrong turn will raise alarm.
So let's embrace this merry chase,
And join the forest's jolly race!

Soft Calls of the Nightingale

Night's singer hums a silly tune,
As fireflies twirl beneath the moon.
A raccoon wearing shades of flair,
Takes center stage with comic air.

A tortoise joins, slow and plump,
Making sure he gets a bump.
While owls roll their big round eyes,
At all the fun beneath the skies.

Crickets chirp in disco beat,
While shadows sway in rhythm sweet.
A dance-off brews among the leaves,
Nature's jesters play their reprieves.

Then nightingale, perched on a branch,
Sings "Join us, folks, let's take a chance!"
With laughter echoed all around,
In this wild night, joy is found!

Tales Woven in Wildflowers

In a meadow bright and bold,
Daisies spin their tales of old.
Butterflies pretzel into knots,
Telling stories that hit the spots.

Honeybees buzz with glee and zest,
Joking as they build their nest.
A dandelion takes a bow,
Sprouting wishes, singing "Wow!"

Petals flutter like aged cards,
While squirrels race and play their guards.
Chasing dreams through blooms they dash,
Under the skies, in a colorful splash.

Each flower whispers secret fun,
While bees and blooms together run.
Nature's laughter fills the air,
In the tapestry of flowers fair!

The Language of the Dappled Glade

In the glade where sunlight beams,
Trees converse in giggly schemes.
Mushrooms sport their polka dots,
While snails play games—oh, what a plot!

With painted leaves like banners bright,
They dance around, a joyful sight.
A chipmunk juggles acorns round,
While shy shadows twirl to the sound.

The breeze brings tales from far and wide,
As playful critters take their ride.
Under canopies of green and gold,
The glade's laughter never gets old.

So come and join this lively place,
Where every creature wears a face.
With chuckles echoed all around,
In this forest, joy is found!

The Enigma of the Leafy Canopy

Under branches thick and green,
A squirrel thinks he's quite a queen.
He chatters loud, just like a fool,
    Claiming acorns as his rule.

A pinecone drops, it hits his head,
"Who tossed that?" he yells, filled with dread.
His crown is gone, but ego's high,
"Next time I'll dodge, I swear, oh my!"

The leaves all rustle, gossip flows,
The chipmunks laugh, as laughter grows.
"Hey buddy, watch out for that tree!"
Squirrel grins back, "They're all jealous of me!"

Underneath the leafy crown,
The forest chatters, no one frowns.
For every nut and every laugh,
Life in the trees is quite the gaffe!

Sotto Voce Under the Stars

The owl hoots, it's time to play,
While raccoons plot their sneaky way.
"Let's raid the picnic!" one raccoon smirks,
"Those ants will never see our quirks!"

The stars twinkle, as if they know,
The antics unfold, a wild show.
"Pass the chips, and don't you dare!
I'll guard the dips with utmost flair!"

A bear stumbles, in search of snacks,
He slips and rolls, oh what a knack!
"Be gentle, folks! I'm on a diet,"
The raccoons laugh, "How can they try it?"

In shadows deep, schemes take flight,
Furry friends laugh deep into night.
Each critter finding joy and fun,
In the great outdoors, no need to run!

Echoing Footfalls on Soft Soil

Each step we take, the earth does giggle,
The rabbits join in, a funny wiggle.
With every thump, a dance begins,
Chasing shadows with their chins.

A turtle trails behind the pack,
"Slow down, pals! You'll hit a rock!"
He bursts forth loud, but time won't bend,
"Wait up! I'm not just here to send!"

The fox leaps high, a nimble sprite,
"Catch me if you can—oh what a sight!"
But as he bounds, he trips on grass,
His friends all snicker, "Oh what a pass!"

The forest floor, a stage so grand,
Each paw and foot, a silly band.
With laughter echoes, joy's a goal,
As critters prance, they steal the soul!

The Unheard Chorus of the Briars

In tangled thickets, where no one dares,
The briars gossip, sharing flares.
A butterfly lands, and they all cheer,
"Quick! Hide the snacks, the humans are near!"

The thorns complain of folks who poke,
With curious hands, they often choke.
"Keep it down, we must stay stealth,"
And off they roll to save their health.

A bushy tail waves, "I know a trick!
Let's close our eyes and play hide and seek!"
But each time they play, the game's quite short,
When tumbleweeds join, it's chaos, not sport!

So in silence, the whispers glide,
Through tangled vines, they all abide.
Each thorny laugh, a secret light,
In the briar's heart, they find delight!

Sylvan Reflections in Still Water

In the glade, squirrels play hide and seek,
Trees giggle as branches gently creak.
A frog croaks jokes, he thinks he's a star,
While butterflies dance, oh, how bizarre!

The brook chuckles, trickling without a care,
As daisies nod, caught in the laughter air.
A bear tumbles down, quite a silly sight,
All of nature bursts into pure delight!

Beneath the roots, ants march in a line,
Carrying crumbs they think are divine.
But who knew leaves were such crafty thieves?
Each laugh echoes, hidden in the eaves!

The moon peeks in, with a grin on her face,
As shadows join in a comical race.
In the end, it's just one big jest,
Nature's humor puts all hearts to the test!

Traces of Dreams in the Understory

Beneath the ferns where the critters collide,
A rabbit tells tales with hilarious pride.
The mushrooms can giggle, you wouldn't believe,
As the wind plays tricks, it's hard to conceive!

A snail on a leaf, with a crown made of dew,
Slow-mo moves like he's got something to prove.
The beetles are ballroom dancing tonight,
With a frog DJ spinning tunes in delight!

A rustle reveals, a prankster raccoon,
Swapping all acorns beneath the full moon.
The shadows are laughing as slide-whistles squeal,
In this little kingdom, what's fake seems so real!

So if you stroll down this odd forest lane,
Look for the giggles and don't miss the train.
Each petal and twig holds a story to tell,
Life's funny in nature, where all hearts dwell!

Echoes Beneath the Canopy

In the high branches where the squirrels convene,
They plot a surprise with acorns obscene.
A parrot squawks jokes, no one finds them lame,
While shadows just chuckle, playing their game!

With every rustle, the leaves form a band,
A chorus of giggles that spread across land.
The owls read fortunes, and they can't stop snickering,
As badger and fox start their unending bickering!

Down below, the mushrooms giggle in pairs,
As raccoons dance under the moonlit flares.
Every flutter brings gleeful surprises,
As fireflies wink, dressed in their disguises!

So step lightly here, join the fun and the cheer,
Where laughter and nature dance oh-so near.
In this forest of joy, every heart finds a tune,
Embrace the humor born under the moon!

Secrets Beneath the Leaves

Underleaf laughter where the hedgehogs roam,
Trees whisper secrets, but they can't find a home.
A chipmunk in shades sings a silly old song,
While the owls hoot loudly, 'Can this be wrong?'

The vines entwine, as the rabbits burst through,
Playing hopscotch on paths only they knew.
Fungi are giggling, they think they're so sly,
While butterflies wear their finest bow tie!

A woodpecker knocks, but it's more of a beat,
And the crickets join in with a tap-tap retreat.
So gather your joys and dance with delight,
In this leafy haven, where laughter takes flight!

So venture with glee, where the funny folks dwell,
Amongst all the secrets that nature will tell.
Under these leaves, keep your heart light and free,
For the comedy here is as grand as can be!

Rustic Reveries in the Twilight

In the twilight glow, the critters chime,
Squirrels gossip about the pace of time.
Come one, come all, to the warm picnic scene,
Where raccoons dance in their fancy cuisine.

Beneath the stars, the frogs serenade,
While owls debate the best way they played.
Bunnies hop, while the fireflies blink,
All laughing loudly, or so one would think.

The Lullaby of the Moonlit Thicket

Beneath the moon, the porcupines strut,
With quills like crowns, they're in quite a rut.
The badgers boast of their burrowed retreats,
While the owlets snack on their late-night sweets.

A raccoon croons that he lost his right shoe,
But don't worry, his hat's quite a view!
The shadows giggle under leafy rafts,
In this moonlit thicket, joy's the best craft.

Serene Conversations Among the Trees

The pines engage in a chirpy debate,
About which tree's tallest and which ones can skate.
The sturdy oaks chuckle at all the fuss,
While the lilacs laugh at this comical bus.

A woodpecker drums on a trunk with glee,
Counting the notes as one, two, and three.
Beetles parade with tiny top hats,
Flaunting their style like fashionable rats.

Treetop Whispers at Dawn

As dawn breaks through, the crows start to squawk,
Plotting their antics on an old tree's dock.
The squirrels scamper, their tails turned high,
Chasing each other, as the sun says hi.

The chipmunks toast with acorns in paws,
Announcing the day with their little "Huzzah!"
With laughter and chirps, the forest awakes,
In this jokey realm, no one ever fakes.

The Hidden Chorus of the Foliage

In the trees, the squirrels debate,
Who takes the last acorn — it's fate!
Frogs croak loudly, they're clearly in charge,
While rabbits plot snacks — they all find it large.

Leaves rustle gently, a giggle or two,
As chipmunks trade secrets and mischief in queue.
A bear strolls by, with a confused little frown,
Wondering why everyone's wearing a crown.

Underfoot, the ants hold a grand parade,
On a crumb they've found, they'll not be delayed.
The hedgehogs are rolling, all tumbled and snug,
While ladybugs laugh — it's all quite a hug.

As dusk tiptoes in, the parties don't stop,
Ghosts of laughter linger, they bob and they hop!
In this merry madness, the moon joins the spree,
And the hidden chorus sets everyone free.

Gazes Shared Among the Roots

Beneath the surface where secrets abound,
The roots hold conferences, quietly profound.
A gopher recites his favorite old tale,
While mushrooms nod off, swaying delicately pale.

Rabbits exchange winks with a sly little grin,
As the daisies spread rumors — let the drama begin!
Worms twist and turn, plotting mischief in style,
While nearby, a deer takes a moment to smile.

The breeze hums softly; it tickles the leaves,
As crickets tune up for their nightly reprieves.
A snail claims a podium, quite proud and robust,
Saying, "Slow and steady? It's all about trust!"

And just when you think the fun's at an end,
A raccoon appears, your unlikeliest friend.
With a cap and a bowtie, he's here for a laugh,
Making sure every root joins the musical path.

The Warmth of Sunlit Silence

In the sunny glades where the shadows play,
The bees do the cha-cha, brightening the day.
A snail takes a selfie — oh what a sight!
While grasshoppers practice their steps in delight.

The daisies are gossiping, sharing a joke,
While butterflies twirl, in colorful cloak.
A shy little hedgehog is counting to ten,
"When I find my friends, we can party again!"

A family of turtles floats by on a log,
Taking their time, quite slower than fog.
The sun winks brightly, the rays fit just right,
In this sunlit silence, there's always a bite.

As shadows stretch long and the day starts to hum,
The frogs feel the beat underneath their green drum.
And they croak out a tune that can't help but cheer,
A celebration of life, every day of the year!

Echoes of Longing Under the Starry Canopy

Under the stars, where the critters all meet,
A fox with a mustache taps his little feet.
The owls share stories that make everyone sigh,
While fireflies twinkle, like stars in the sky.

Nights filled with dreams, the glowworms unite,
A party in shadows, all dancing in light.
A raccoon in a cape claims the title of king,
As the starlight invites them to join in the swing!

Beneath the vastness, the crickets compose,
A melody sweet that nobody knows.
The hedgehogs debate the best shape for a dance,
While bats swoop low, chasing dreams in a trance.

And as dawn approaches with a sleepy goodbye,
The laughter emerges like mist from the sky.
Under this canopy, aching to play,
The echoes of longing will stay night and day.

www.ingramcontent.com/pod-product-compliance
Lightning Source LLC
Chambersburg PA
CBHW071830160426
43209CB00003B/264